THE UNITED STATES BEFORE THE CIVIL WAR

KaaVonia Hinton

Children's Press®
An imprint of Scholastic Inc.

Special thanks to our consultant, Dr. Le'Trice Donaldson, Assistant Professor of History, Auburn University, for making sure the text of the book is authentic and historically accurate.

Thanks also to our sensitivity readers, Aaron Talley, a Chicago public school teacher, and Deirdre Lynn Hollman, Senior Curriculum Specialist from the Black Education Research Center at Teachers College, Columbia University, for making sure the content of this book is appropriate for school instruction.

Library of Congress Cataloging-in-Publication Data available

ISBN 978-1-5461-3631-6 (library binding) | ISBN 978-1-5461-3632-3 (paperback) |
ISBN 978-1-5461-3633-0 (ebook)

10 9 8 7 6 5 4 3 2 1 25 26 27 28 29

Printed in China 62
First edition, 2025

Design by Kathleen Petelinsek
Series produced by Spooky Cheetah Press

Front cover: An enslaved family on a plantation in South Carolina

Back cover: Harvesting cotton

Find the Truth!

Everything you are about to read is true ***except*** for one of the sentences on this page.

Which one is **TRUE**?

T or F There weren't any enslaved people in the Northern United States in 1800.

T or F President Thomas Jefferson enslaved more than 600 people in his life.

Find the answers in this book.

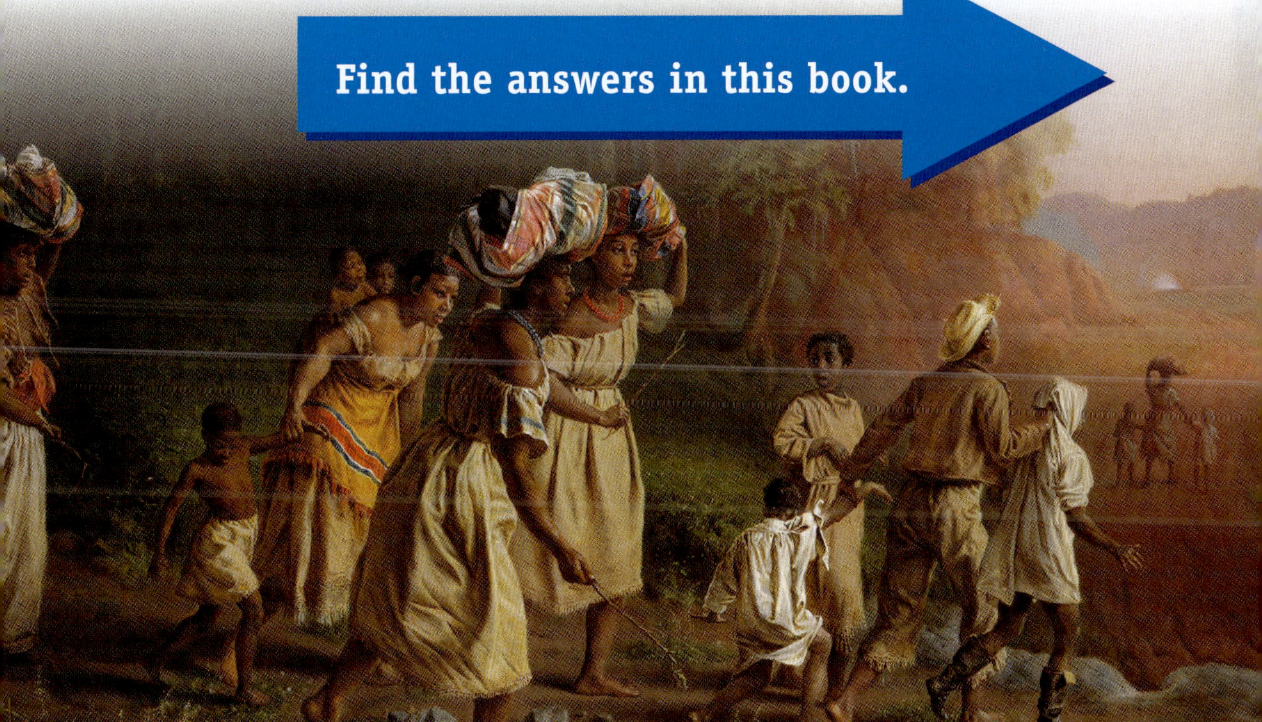

What's in This Book?

Introduction 6

1 Slavery in the 13 Colonies

How did slavery begin in the British colonies in North America? 9

2 Slavery in the South

What was the experience of enslaved people in the South? 15

Many enslaved people in the South labored on large farms called plantations.

Indigenous Peoples in the Southeast were forced from their homelands to make room for plantations.

Enslaved People Fought Back

How did enslaved people resist slavery? 22

3 Slavery in the North

How was slavery profitable for Northerners? 25

4 The Road to War

What events led to the Civil War? 31

People to Know 40
Eyewitness to History 42
True Statistics 44
Resources 45
Glossary 46
Index 47
About the Author 48

CAUTION!!
COLORED PEOPLE
OF BOSTON, ONE & ALL,
You are hereby respectfully CAUTIONED and advised, to avoid conversing with the
Watchmen and Police Officers of Boston,
For since the recent ORDER OF THE MAYOR & ALDERMEN, they are empowered to act as
KIDNAPPERS
AND
Slave Catchers,
And they have already been actually employed in KIDNAPPING, CATCHING, AND KEEPING SLAVES. Therefore, if you value your LIBERTY, and the *Welfare of the Fugitives* among you, *Shun* them in every possible manner, as so many *HOUNDS* on the track of the most unfortunate of your race.
Keep a Sharp Look Out for KIDNAPPERS, and have TOP EYE open.
APRIL 24, 1851.

A poster warns fugitives from slavery about people who will try to capture them in the North.

INTRODUCTION

In **1783**, the 13 British colonies in North America **became a new country**: the United States of America. Soon after, leaders from **12 of the 13** states met to write the U.S. Constitution. Although they were part of one country, each state the leaders represented was unique. They were **different geographically**. They had **different resources** and ways of life. They also had **different views** on **slavery**.

This painting shows the signing of the U.S. Constitution in 1787.

In the **South**, most white people wanted to continue this unjust and **cruel practice**. The region's **economy** was dependent on it. It provided **immense wealth** for enslavers. In the North and Midwest, many people wanted to **slow the expansion of slavery**. Some wanted to **abolish**, or end, it completely. The leaders who met to write the Constitution made **compromises** about slavery. However, the practice continued to **cause tension** in the nation for years. These tensions ultimately **threatened the country's very existence**.

Indigenous Peoples were the first to be enslaved in the North American colonies.

Some of the first Africans arrived in the Americas in the late 1400s. They were explorers who worked for the Spanish government.

The first enslaved Africans in the British colonies in North America arrive at Jamestown in 1619.

CHAPTER

Slavery in the 13 Colonies

In 1619, the first enslaved Africans arrived at Jamestown in the British colony of Virginia. An English ship captain traded them for food and supplies. In 1640, a Black man named John Punch became the first documented person in the colonies to be enslaved for life. Then, in 1641, Massachusetts became the first of the original 13 British colonies to legalize the institution of slavery. What would one day become the United States was now part of the transatlantic slave trade.

Dangerous Voyage

As part of the transatlantic slave trade, European enslavers kidnapped Black men, women, and children from their homes in Africa to sell them in the Americas. These people, who might have been teachers, doctors, or community leaders in their native towns, were then chained together and forced to march hundreds of miles to the coast, where they were packed tightly onto ships. Nearly half of all captured Africans died on the journey from their homes to the Americas.

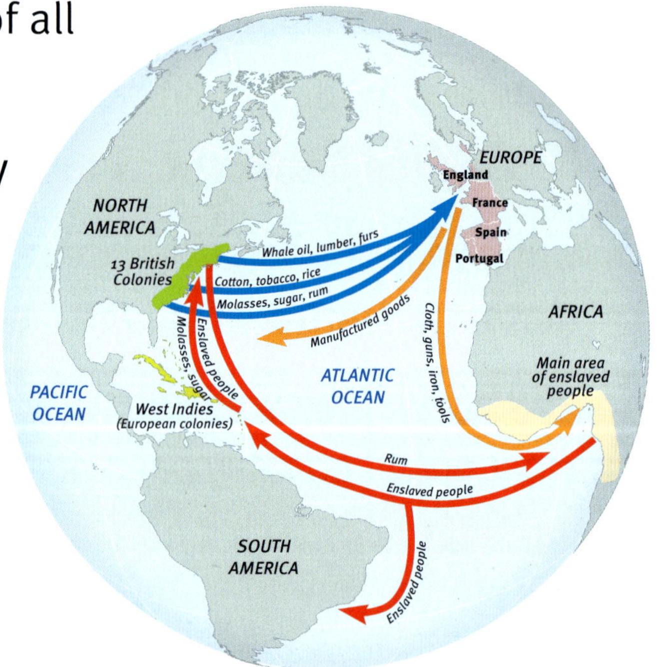

The transatlantic slave trade was part of the larger triangular trade shown on this map.

Enslaved people were considered property—not people—and were treated as such.

In an auction, enslaved people were sold to the person willing to pay the most.

Up for Auction

Upon their arrival in the colonies, captive people were sold in auctions to the highest bidder. As they stood on a platform, enslavers would inspect their teeth and limbs in order to draw conclusions about their health and their ability to work long hours. Families were torn apart, with mothers, fathers, and siblings being sold to different people. People from the same or neighboring African villages and those who spoke the same language were often separated.

One law made it illegal for enslaved people to learn to read or write.

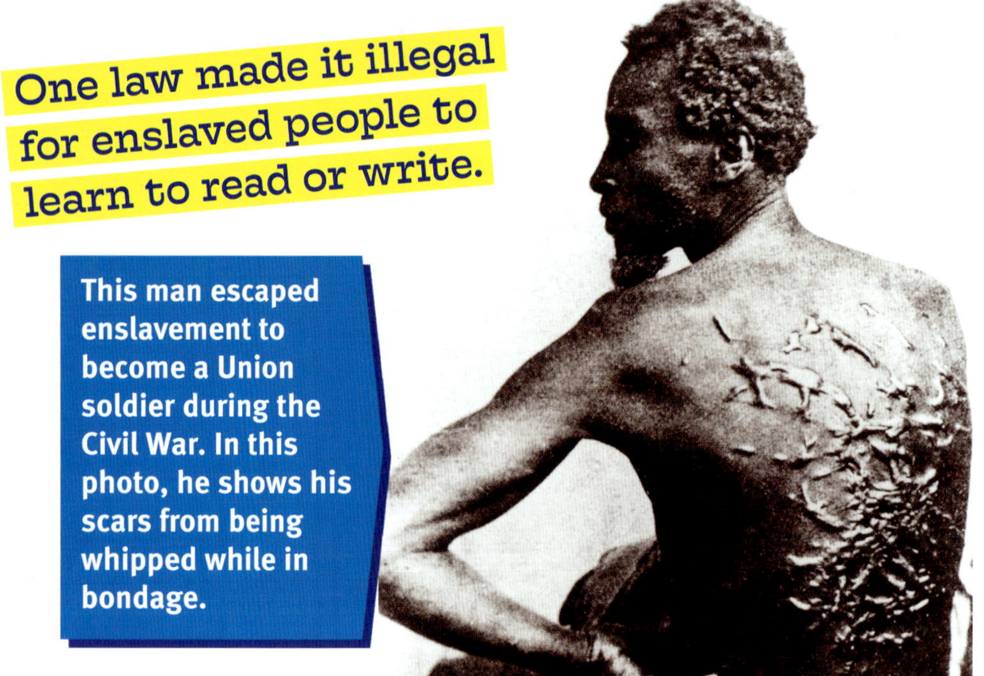

This man escaped enslavement to become a Union soldier during the Civil War. In this photo, he shows his scars from being whipped while in bondage.

Controlling Enslaved People

By the early 1700s, enslaved Black people in some colonies began to outnumber white Americans. Frightened colonizers passed laws to control them. An enslaved person who broke a law would be beaten or even killed. This happened in front of the other captive people. Their enslavers wanted to scare them into obeying the rules. That is one reason the institution of slavery was able to continue for so long.

Enslavement usually lasted a person's entire life—and any children they had were enslaved too. That is why the number of enslaved people in the United States steadily increased through the 1700s and even after 1808, when it became illegal to import enslaved people from other countries.

The threat of sale to another part of the state or country was used to control enslaved people.

In 1850, the South had about 75,000 cotton plantations.

Cotton was the most important **cash crop** in the South.

CHAPTER

Slavery in the South

By the early 1800s, the Southern economy had become dependent on agriculture, especially valuable crops like sugar, cotton, and tobacco. As colonizers had settled in colonies in the South, they had forced Indigenous Peoples from their homelands. The white settlers built small farms as well as large farms called plantations, where enslaved people were forced to live and work for no pay. This cheap form of labor made many plantation owners wealthy.

Working in the Fields

The experience of enslaved people could be very different depending on the place and time they were enslaved, as well their gender and age. On a plantation, for example, some of the enslaved workers labored in the fields—including children as young as five years old. The people toiled six days a week, from sunup until sundown, whether the temperatures were scorching hot or freezing cold.

After a woman gave birth, she had to carry the baby on her back into the fields to work.

More than half of all enslaved people in the South worked on cotton plantations.

White farmers and workers also worked on large plantations. But they were paid for their labor.

The actual work done by enslaved people in the fields varied based on the type of crops that were grown. But no matter the crop, enslaved people prepared the ground for planting, planted the seeds, cared for the crops, and then harvested them. Many plantations had overseers who punished people if they did not work or if they worked slowly.

Enslaved servants had to be available to their enslavers 24 hours a day.

Working in Homes

Some of the enslaved people on a plantation worked in the house. They cooked, served meals, and cleaned. They took care of the plantation owner's family—including bathing and dressing them. Enslaved children often had to serve as playmates while attending to the needs of white children.

Enslaved people who worked in the home rarely had time to spend with their own families.

Special Skills, Trades, and Talents

Many enslaved people had special skills or worked in a specific trade. For example, some women made clothing for the plantation owners' families or worked as nurses. Some men were blacksmiths, who made objects like horseshoes, weapons, and chains. Others were carpenters and bricklayers, constructing and maintaining buildings. Sometimes these skilled laborers were paid for their work. A very few were able to save up enough money to buy their freedom.

This woman is spinning cotton into yarn to be used for clothing.

Some enslaved people planted gardens and raised chickens because enslavers did not give them much to eat.

Enslaved people usually lived in shacks with dirt floors and slept on beds of straw. Most were not given shoes. They had few clothes.

Hope in Scarcity

Enslaved people were not legally allowed to marry, but they still built loving families. However, they lived with the constant fear of being separated from their loved ones. Despite all these hardships, they fought to maintain their very diverse African cultures including their own music, languages, crafts, and religious practices. They also created new traditions. They continued to have hopes and dreams.

Indian Removal

Plantation owners who got rich from the labor of enslaved workers wanted more land to plant more crops. In the South that meant taking even more land from the Indigenous Peoples living there. In 1830, President Andrew Jackson signed the Indian Removal Act into law. The law allowed him to force Cherokee, Choctaw, Chickasaw, Muscogee (Creek), and Seminole nations off their land in the Southeast and move them west. The Cherokee people challenged the law and won. The U.S. Supreme Court ruled that they could not be forced to move. However, Jackson made an illegal treaty that resulted in the Cherokees' removal in 1838. About 100,000 Indigenous people were forced to walk thousands of miles to their new lands. Along the way, thousands died from disease, starvation, and extreme temperatures.

A small number of free Black and Indigenous Peoples were enslavers.

The Cherokees' forced relocation came to be known as the Trail of Tears.

The **BIG** Truth

Enslaved People Fought Back

White enslavers believed they were superior to the Black people they enslaved. That was one excuse they used to justify this practice. Some also claimed that enslaved people were happy and better off having enslavers to take care of them. But the idea of "happy slaves" is a lie. Enslaved people wanted to be free. They tried to gain their freedom in many ways.

BREAKING FREE

Captives resisted from the moment they were kidnapped in Africa. Some people tried to fight off the kidnappers or break away when they were being transported to the coast. Once on the ship, some captive people fought the crew and tried to take over the ship.

Rather than live a life in bondage, some enslaved people jumped from ships into the ocean.

LEARNING TO READ AND WRITE

Literacy was an important form of resistance. Enslaved people who could read were introduced to ideas written by people who were fighting to end slavery, called abolitionists. Enslaved people could also get access to information about how they could reach free states. Literate enslaved people occasionally wrote notes that helped in their own escape.

TAKING THE UNDERGROUND RAILROAD

Many freedom seekers escaped slavery using the Underground Railroad, a secret network of abolitionists. Most secrets about how to leave the plantation in the middle of the night were in codes like songs, knocking patterns, or written notes. Once on the Underground Railroad, enslaved people were guided and hidden in safe spaces.

REBELLING

Some enslaved people led armed revolts against their oppressors. In 1831, Nat Turner (pictured) led one of the deadliest revolts in the United States. Turner's group of about 70 freedom seekers killed 57 white people before the revolt ended. Turner was eventually captured and hanged. White people killed about 200 Black people in revenge, though many were not involved in the revolt.

Enslaved men worked on the docks in the Northeast's many port cities.

The last enslaved person in New York state was not freed until 1827.

CHAPTER

Slavery in the North

By the early 1800s, the North had a largely **industrial** economy. This part of the country had fewer enslaved people than the South. In the North, enslaved people worked on small farms and in homes, factories, and mills. Some were seamen or worked in taverns, inns, and stores.

By 1804, all states in the North had enacted gradual **emancipation** laws. They would start phasing out slavery a little at a time.

Profiting from Slavery

Even in places where slavery was ultimately outlawed, the region still benefited from the practice. Banks and insurance companies in the North financed slave traders, plantation owners, and others involved in slavery. Some of the cotton produced by enslaved people in the South was used in **textile** mills in the North. Many mills produced rough cloth, which was used to make clothes for the enslaved.

There were cases of free Black people in the North being kidnapped and sold into slavery.

Workers in this Northern textile mill spin cotton from the South into yarn to be used in fabric.

Fugitive Slave Laws

Many freedom seekers fled to states in the North that had outlawed slavery, but the region was not completely safe for them—or the people who helped them. The Fugitive Slave Act of 1793 was a law that said freedom seekers who entered states or territories where slavery was illegal would be returned to enslavers. Anyone who tried to assist them would be fined. The Fugitive Slave Act of 1850 was harsher. It said citizens in states or territories where slavery was illegal could not assist enslaved people—and they were required to help enslavers recapture freedom seekers.

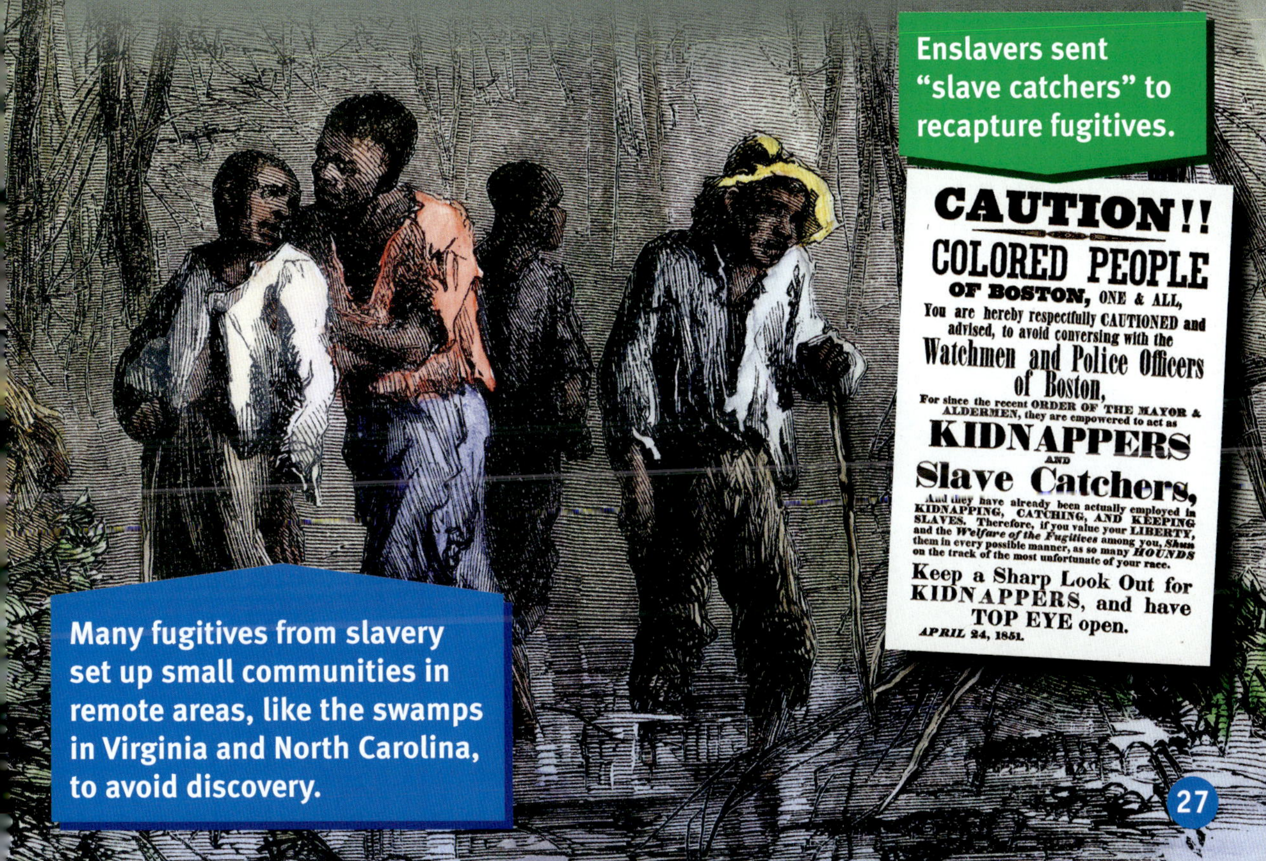

Enslavers sent "slave catchers" to recapture fugitives.

Many fugitives from slavery set up small communities in remote areas, like the swamps in Virginia and North Carolina, to avoid discovery.

Working to End Slavery

People in the abolitionist movement (also known as the antislavery movement) thought enslavement was morally wrong, and they worked to end it. They included white people as well as free Black people. Abolitionists pressured Northern states to end slavery. Many were part of the Underground Railroad.

Quakers were among the first religious groups to forbid members from enslaving people.

This house, which belonged to Levi and Catherine Coffin, was a stop on the Underground Railroad in Indiana.

Frederick Douglass at a convention with other abolitionists in 1850

Abolitionists were often threatened, hurt, and killed because they tried to end slavery. Some abolitionists, like Frederick Douglass, had escaped slavery and spoke out about the cruelty of bondage, even though doing so put them in danger.

Southern plantation owners rushed to claim fertile land in America's growing Western territories.

This sugarcane plantation is in Louisiana, which was originally part of a territory that allowed slavery.

CHAPTER

The Road to War

The country began growing soon after the Revolutionary War ended in 1783. As states were added to the nation, government leaders had to decide whether slavery would be allowed there. Several presidents were enslavers, as were other lawmakers and Supreme Court justices, and they supported expanding slavery.

Rules were created for how territories could apply to become states. Many lawmakers believed each state should decide if slavery would be allowed there. But there were also expectations about limiting the expansion of slavery.

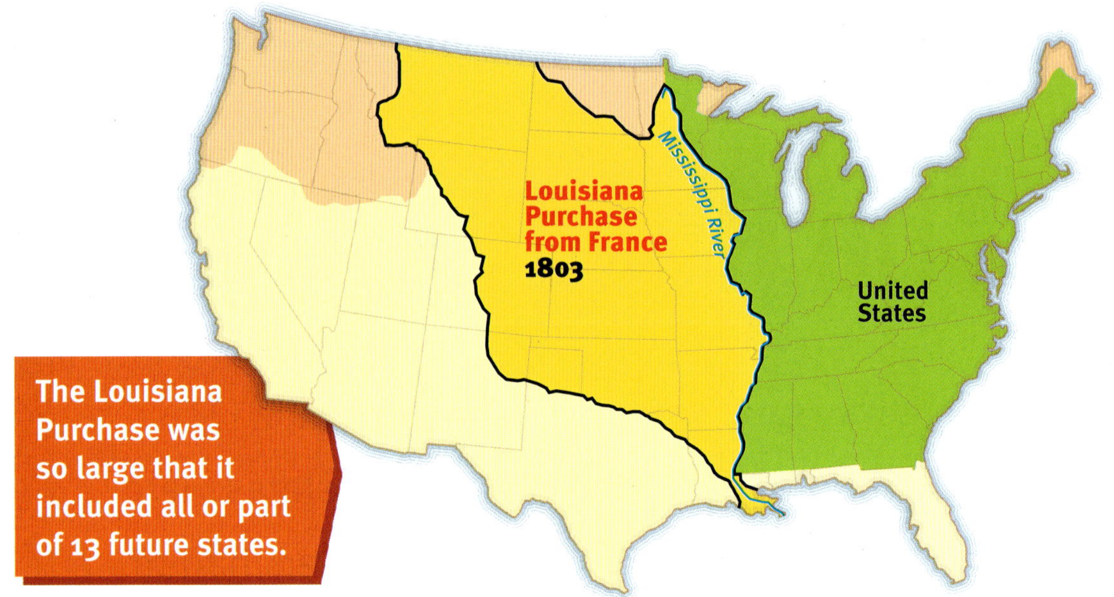

The Largest Land Purchase

In 1802, the United States reached only as far west as the Mississippi River, and Americans were anxious for the country to grow. They believed in the idea of Manifest Destiny—that America was destined to stretch from the Atlantic Ocean to the Pacific. At the time, other parts of the continent were controlled by France and Spain.

Then, in 1803, President Thomas Jefferson purchased the Louisiana Territory from France. The purchase almost doubled the country's size. Jefferson, who was an enslaver, said slavery would be legal in the new territory. Many Southern plantation owners moved into the area and brought their enslaved workers with them.

Thomas Jefferson owned more than 600 enslaved people throughout his life.

Meriwether Lewis (center) and William Clark led an expedition across America's newly acquired lands. Sacagawea, a Shoshone woman, was important to the team's success.

Tipping the Balance

In 1812, part of the Louisiana Purchase lands became the Missouri Territory. In 1818, Missouri (MO) applied to become a state that would allow slavery. There were 22 states in the country. Eleven allowed slavery and 11 did not. Northern lawmakers worried that admitting Missouri would upset the balance of power in the government.

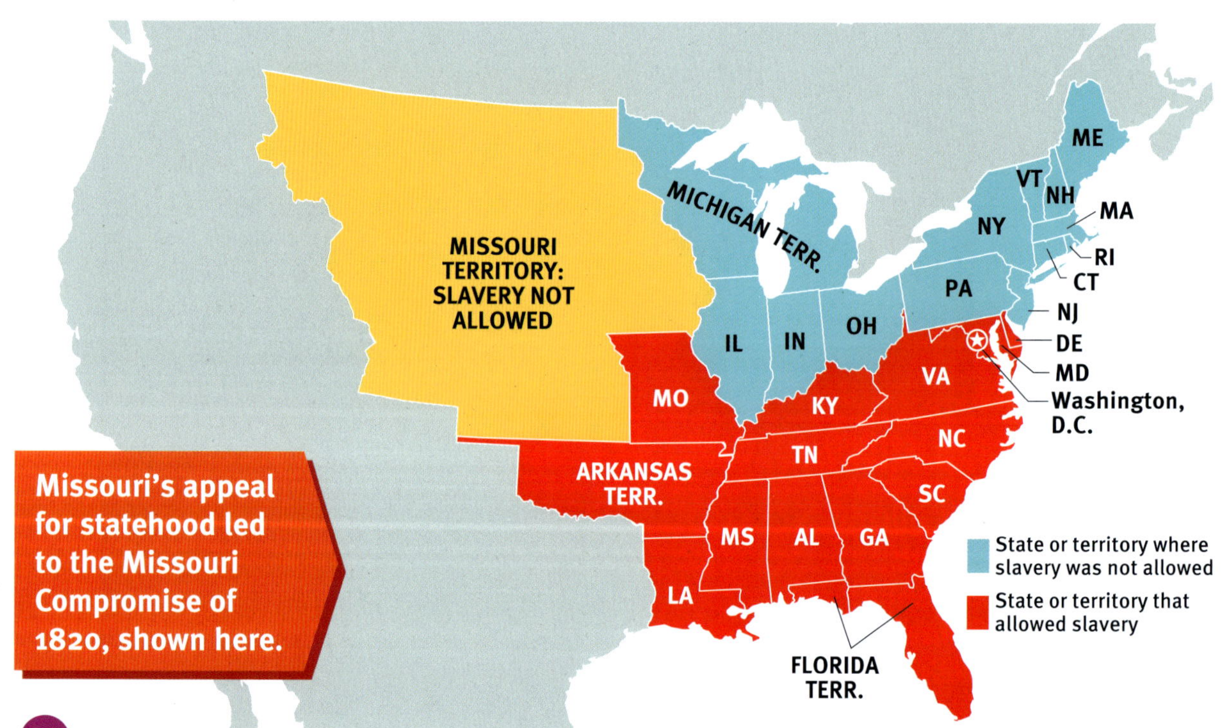

Missouri's appeal for statehood led to the Missouri Compromise of 1820, shown here.

Henry Clay was the architect of the Missouri Compromise.

Before becoming a state, Maine was once part of Massachusetts.

In 1820, Congressman Henry Clay proposed a compromise. The states of Missouri and Maine would be admitted to the Union together. Missouri would allow slavery, and Maine would not. Slavery would also not be allowed in the remaining Missouri Territory. Shortly after, control of the Florida territory moved from Spain to the United States. Slavery was allowed there—but it was not a state yet.

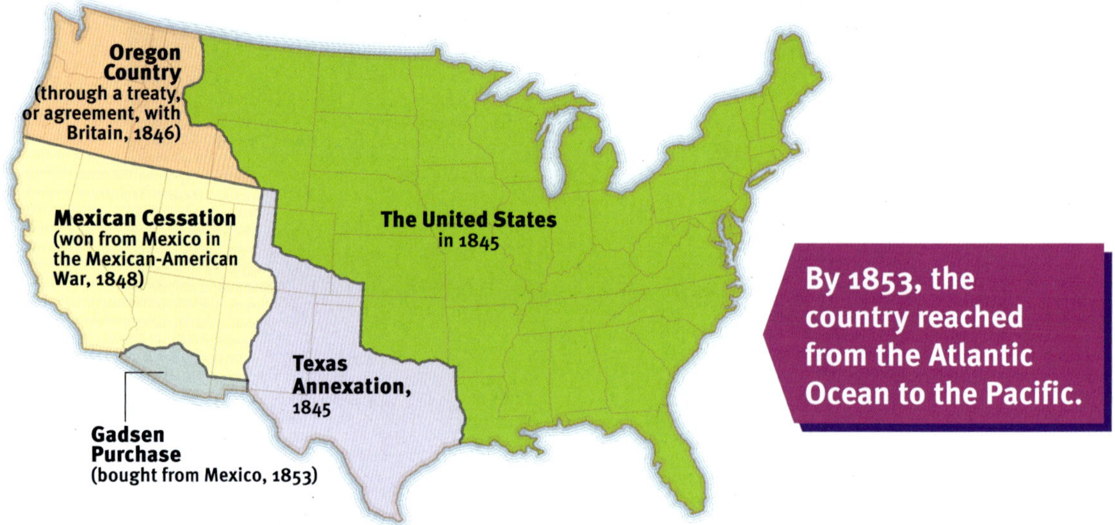

By 1853, the country reached from the Atlantic Ocean to the Pacific.

Sea to Shining Sea

In 1845, the U.S. government increased the size of the country again by **annexing** Texas. A war with Mexico quickly followed, which ended with the United States winning even more land. The country now spread from coast to coast. Tension over slavery increased. Then, in 1854, the Kansas-Nebraska Act canceled the Missouri Compromise. It said leaders of the new territories, not federal lawmakers, should decide if slavery would be allowed. The act also allowed slavery in the remaining part of the Missouri Territory.

No More than Property

Dred Scott was an enslaved man living in the state of Missouri, where slavery was legal. His enslavers took him to Illinois and the Wisconsin Territory, where slavery was against the law. In 1846, after Scott and his enslavers returned to Missouri, Scott sued for his freedom. According to the Missouri courts, if an enslaved person was taken to a free state or territory, he was freed—even if he returned to Missouri. Scott's case went all the way to the U.S. Supreme Court, which is the highest court in the land. In 1857, the justices ruled that Black people, including free Black people, could not be United States citizens. Therefore they had no right to sue. Scott remained in bondage.

A bronze statue of Dred Scott and his wife, Harriet, in front of the Old Courthouse in St. Louis, Missouri

Formation of the Republican Party

The heated debate over the spread of slavery led to the formation of a new political party. In 1854, the early Republican Party was formed to stop the spread of slavery. Republicans were not necessarily abolitionists. They did not want slavery to spread because it provided unpaid labor. That meant there were fewer jobs available for white workers.

Timeline: Slavery Before Secession

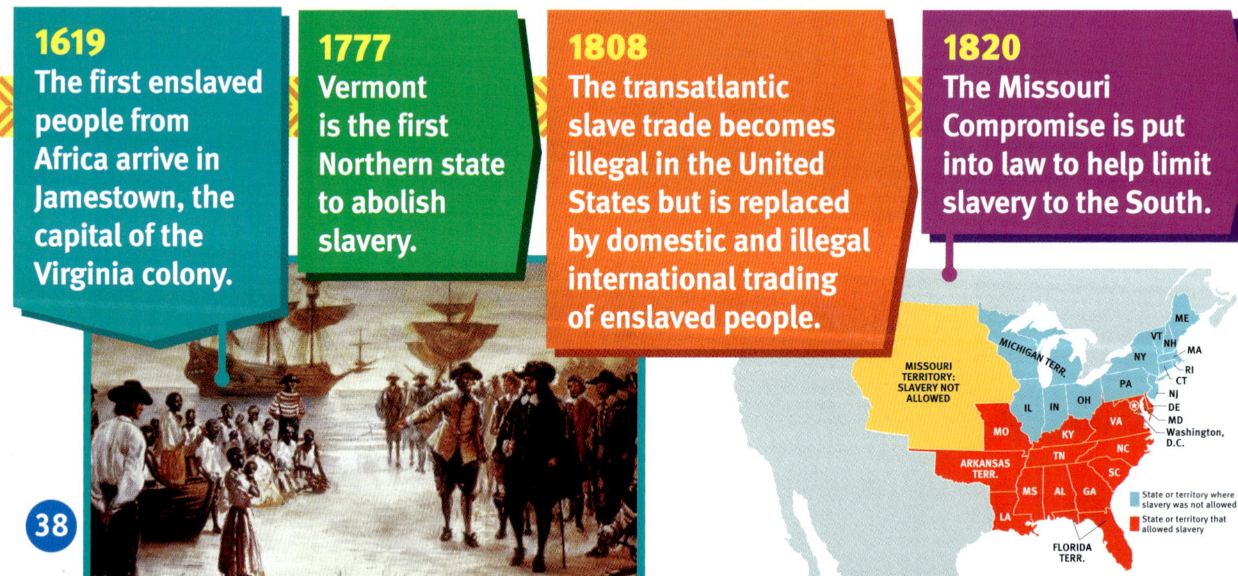

The Beginning of the End

About four million people were enslaved in the United States before the Civil War.

In November 1860, Republican Abraham Lincoln was elected president. White Southern politicians feared slavery would end. In December 1860, South Carolina **seceded**, or left the Union, and other Southern states followed. By the time Lincoln was **inaugurated** in March 1861, seven states had seceded and attempted to form their own country: the Confederate States of America. Before long, the nation would be at war.

1830
The forced removal of Cherokee, Chickasaw, Choctaw, Muscogee (Creek), and Seminole nations from their homelands begins.

1850
The Fugitive Slave Act of 1850 is passed to return freedom seekers to slavery.

TWO HUNDRED DOLLARS

REWARD!

Ran away from the subscriber, on the 6th inst., my boy Manuel. He is about 35 years of age, about 5 feet 7 inches high, heavy built weighing about 160 pounds. He has a shrewd expression of the eye, and has a scar on one of his thighs occasioned from a burn, is well

1854
The Kansas-Nebraska Act repeals the Missouri Compromise and expands slavery.

1860
Abraham Lincoln is elected president and Southern secession begins. The American Civil War starts a few months later, in April 1861.

People to Know

John Brown
(1800–1859)

Brown was an abolitionist who led a raid on the federal arsenal—a place where weapons are stored—at Harpers Ferry, Virginia, in 1859. His plan was to lead a rebellion to liberate enslaved people. Brown's mission failed and he was hanged by the authorities.

Elizabeth Freeman
(1742?–1829)

In 1781, Freeman successfully sued for her freedom by claiming slavery was illegal according to the Massachusetts Constitution. Once freed, she changed her name from Mum Bett to Elizabeth Freeman. Her case sparked others and led Massachusetts to end slavery.

William Lloyd Garrison
(1805–1879)

Garrison was an activist whose newspaper, *The Liberator*, published antislavery ideas. He believed enslaved people should be liberated and treated equally. For a few years, Garrison worked with Frederick Douglass to fight slavery.

Sojourner Truth
(1797–1883)

Truth was born Isabella Baumfree in New York. After gaining her freedom, Truth became an abolitionist and activist who gave speeches all over the country during a time when few women did so. In 1828, Truth sued for her son's freedom and won.

Harriet Tubman
(1821?–1913)

Tubman, who was born Araminta Ross, escaped slavery in Maryland and became part of the Underground Railroad. Even though rewards were offered for her capture, Tubman returned to the South many times to help others escape.

Angelina Grimké Weld
(1805–1879)

Weld, a white woman who grew up on a plantation in South Carolina, was a vocal abolitionist. In 1836, she published a pamphlet, *Appeal to the Christian Women of the South*, in which she encouraged other women to join the antislavery movement.

Eyewitness to History

Historians use primary sources to study the past. These are documents such as letters, manuscripts, diaries, photographs, and newspaper stories created during the time under study. Here are two primary sources from the United States before the Civil War that offer a glimpse of what life was like back then.

ONA JUDGE was enslaved by U.S. President George Washington and his wife, Martha, in Virginia. The woman, who was called Oney by her enslavers, escaped on May 21, 1796, while the president was away. An ad was placed in the *Philadelphia Gazette* on May 23, 1796, to try to recapture her. The ad was unsuccessful. Judge remained free until her death in 1848.

No. 43, fouth Water ftreet.

May 23 d10t

Advertifement.

ABSCONDED from the houfhold of the Prefident of the United States, ONEY JUDGE, a light mulatto girl, much freckled, with very black eyes and bufhy black hair, fhe is of middle ftature, flender, and delicately formed, about 20 years of age.

She has many changes of good clothes, of all forts, but they are not fufficiently recollected to be defcribed—As there was no fufpicion of her going off, nor no provocation to do fo, it is not eafy to conjecture whither fhe has gone, or fully, what her defign is;— but as fhe may attempt to efcape by water, all mafters of veffels are cautioned againft admitting her into them, although it is probable fhe will attempt to pafs for a free woman, and has, it is faid, wherewithal to pay her paffage.

Ten dollars will be paid to any perfon who will bring her home, if taken in the city, or on board any veffel in the harbour;—and a reafonable additional fum if apprehended at, and brought from a greater diftance, and in proportion to the diftance.

FREDERICK KITT, Steward.

May 23 d2t

The ad from the Philadelphia Gazette

Sarah Frances Shaw Graves was born into slavery in Kentucky in 1850. After she gained her freedom, Graves talked about her experiences with people who were putting together a collection called *Born in Slavery: Slave Narratives from the Federal Writers' Project, 1936 to 1938*. This is part of Graves's story:

We left my papa in Kentucky, 'cause he was allotted to another man. My papa never knew where my mama went, an' my mama never knew where papa went. They never wanted mama to know, 'cause they [knew] she would never marry so long she knew where he was. Our master wanted her to marry again and raise more children to be slaves. They never wanted mama to know where papa was, an' she never did.

Photograph of Sarah Frances Shaw Graves

True Statistics

Estimated length of the journey to transport enslaved people across the Atlantic Ocean: 3 months

Estimated number of African people stolen from their homes during the transatlantic slave trade: 12 million

Estimated number of African people brought to the British colonies in North America and sold into enslavement: 500,000

How long the legal transatlantic slave trade lasted: About 300 years

Estimated number of people Harriet Tubman helped gain freedom: 70

Number of U.S. presidents who enslaved people while in office: 8

Number of years the Missouri Compromise was law: 34

Number of people enslaved in the United States before the Civil War: About 4 million

Did you find the truth?

F There weren't any enslaved people in the Northern United States in 1800.

T President Thomas Jefferson enslaved more than 600 people in his life.

Resources

Other books in this series:

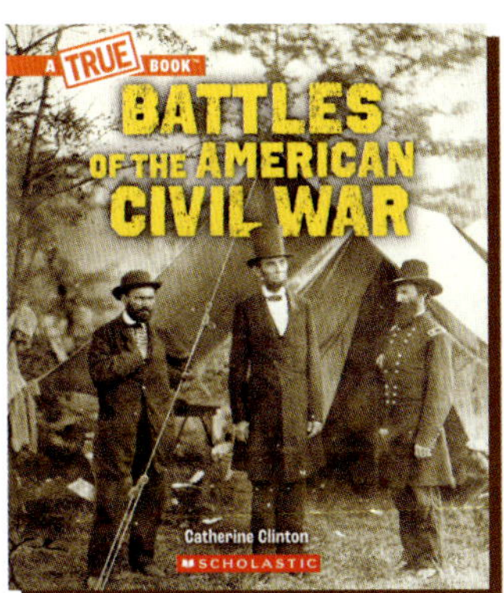

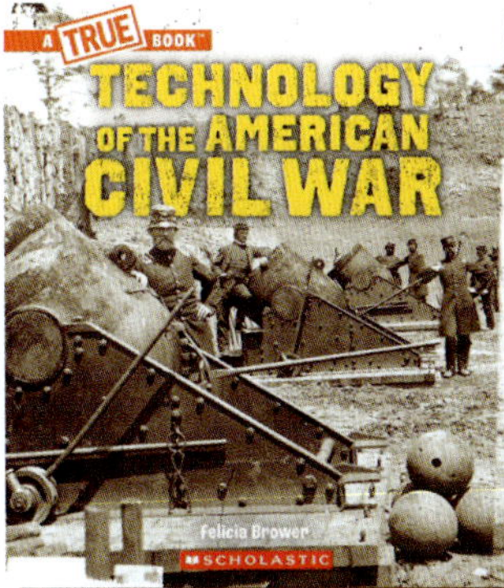

You can also look at:

Benoit, Peter. *The British Colonies in North America*. New York: Children's Press, 2013.

McKissack, Patricia C., and Fredrick McKissack. *Sojourner Truth: Ain't I a Woman*. New York: Scholastic, 1992.

Ribke, Simone T. *Thomas Jefferson* (Rookie Biographies). New York: Children's Press, 2015.

Wilkins, Ebony. *If You Traveled on the Underground Railroad*. Illustrated by Steffi Walthall. New York: Scholastic, 2022.

Glossary

abolish (uh-BAH-lish) to officially do away with

annexing (AN-ek-sing) taking control of a country or territory

cash crop (KASH krahp) a crop, such as cotton or tobacco, that is produced or gathered primarily to be sold

compromises (KAHM-pruh-mizez) agreements that are reached after people with opposing views each give up some of their demands

economy (i-KAH-nuh-mee) the system of buying, selling, making things, and managing money in a place

emancipation (i-man-suh-PAY-shuhn) freedom from enslavement

inaugurated (in-AW-gyuh-ray-ted) sworn into office

Indigenous Peoples (in-DI-juh-nuhs PEE-puhlz) the first known inhabitants of a place

industrial (in-DUHS-tree-uhl) of or having to do with factories and making things in large quantities

seceded (si-SEE-did) formally withdrew from the United States to form another country

slavery (SLAY-vur-ee) the practice of holding people as property against their will, forcing them to work for no pay under threat of violence, and denying them the rights held by free persons

textile (TEK-stile) a woven or knitted fabric or cloth

Index

Page numbers in **bold** indicate illustrations.

abolitionists, 23, 28–29, **28–29**, **38**, 40–41, **40–41**
Africans, enslaved, 8–10, **8**, **10**, **38**
auctions, enslaved people, 11, **11**

British colonies, 6, 8–11, **8–11**, 13, **13**
Brown, John, 40, **40**

Civil War, 39, **39**, 42
Clay, Henry, 35, **35**
cotton, 14–17, **14–17**, 26, **26**

Douglass, Frederick, 29, **29**, 40

enslaved people
  children of, 12, 16, **16**, 18, 20, **20**
  families of, 11, 18, 20, **20**, 43, **43**
  mistreatment of, 10–13, **10–13**
  overview, **38–39**
  resistance of, 22–24, **22–24**, 27, **27**, 37, **37**, 40–42, **40–42**
  sale of, 11, **11**, 12, 20, 26
  skills of, 19, **19**
  work of, 16–19, **16–19**, 24–25, **24**

Freeman, Elizabeth, 40, **40**
fugitive slave laws, 27, **27**, **39**

Garrison, William Lloyd, 40, **40**
Graves, Sarah Frances Shaw, 43, **43**

Indian Removal Act (1830), 21, **21**, **39**
Indigenous Peoples, 7, 15, 21, **21**

Jefferson, Thomas, 33
Judge, Ona, 42, **42**

Kansas-Nebraska Act (1854), 36, 39

Lewis and Clark Expedition, 33, **33**
Lincoln, Abraham, 39, **39**
Louisiana Purchase, 32–33, **32–33**

Missouri Compromise, 34–36, **34–35**, **38–39**

Northern states, 7, 24–30, **24–30**, **34**, **38**

plantations, 14–19, **14–19**, **30**
primary sources, 42–43, **42–43**

reading and writing, 13, 23, **23**
Republican Party, 38–39

Scott, Dred, 37, **37**
slavery, national disagreement about, 7, 31, 34–36, **34–36**, 38–39, **38–39**
slave trade, **8**, 8–10, **10**, 26, **38**
Southern states, 7, 14–21, **14–21**, **30**, **34**, 39, **39**

Truth, Sojourner, 41, **41**
Tubman, Harriet, 41, **41**

Underground Railroad, 23, **23**, 28, **28**, 41
U.S. Constitution, 6, 7, **6–7**

Washington, George, 42, **42**
Weld, Angelina Grimké, 41, **41**
Western territories, 30–36, **30–36**

About the Author

KaaVonia Hinton earned a B.S. and an M.A. from North Carolina Agricultural and Technical State University and a Ph.D. from the Ohio State University. Currently, she is a professor in the Department of Teaching and Learning at Old Dominion University and the author of several nonfiction books for children about United States history, including the Civil War. She feels deeply connected to the first British colonies in the United States, as she grew up in rural North Carolina and lives in Virginia.

Photos ©: back cover: The Miriam and Ira D. Wallach Division of Art, Prints and Photographs/The New York Public Library; 3: Everett/Shutterstock; 4: Wikimedia; 5 top: Winona Nelson; 5 bottom: Library of Congress; 6–7: GraphicaArtis/Getty Images; 8–9: Hulton Archive/Getty Images; 10: Jim McMahon/Mapman®; 11: Universal History Archive/UIG/Shutterstock; 12: North Wind Picture Archives/Alamy Images; 13: The LIFE Picture Collection/Shutterstock; 14–15 main: J. A. Palmer/The Miriam and Ira D. Wallach Division of Art, Prints and Photographs/The New York Public Library; 14 inset: Jim McMahon/Mapman®; 16: Wikimedia; 17: Science History Images/Alamy Images; 18: Lakeview Images/Alamy Images; 19: USWPA/Library of Congress; 20: Fotosearch/Getty Images; 21: Winona Nelson; 22–23 background: Everett/Shutterstock; 22 inset: North Wind Picture Archives/Alamy Images; 23 top inset: FLHC MDB5/Alamy Images; 23 center inset: Greg Copeland; 24–25 main: Bettmann/Getty Images; 24 inset: Jim McMahon/Mapman®; 26: Bettmann/Getty Images; 27 main: North Wind Picture Archives/Alamy Images; 27 inset: Library of Congress; 28: Felix Koch/Cincinnati Museum Center/Getty Images; 29: Fotosearch/Getty Images; 30–31: Walter Bibikow/Jon Arnold Images Ltd/Alamy Images; 32: Jim McMahon/Mapman®; 33: The Granger Collection; 34: Jim McMahon/Mapman®; 35: Volgi archive/Alamy Images; 36: Jim McMahon/Mapman®; 37 inset: Wikimedia; 38 left: Hulton Archive/Getty Images; 38 right: Jim McMahon/Mapman®; 39 left: Winona Nelson; 39 center: Gilder Lehrman Institute of American History/Bridgeman Images; 39 right: Kean Collection/Getty Images; 40 top: Corbis/Getty Images; 40 center: Susan Anne Ridley Sedgwick/Massachusetts Historical Society, Boston/Wikimedia; 40 bottom: Stock Montage/Stock Montage/Getty Images; 41 top: Bettmann/Getty Images; 41 center: Smith Collection/Gado/Getty Images; 41 bottom: Science History Images/Alamy Images; 42 ad: Magite Historic/Alamy Images; 43 right: USWPA/Library of Congress; 44: Kean Collection/Getty Images.

All other photos © Shutterstock.